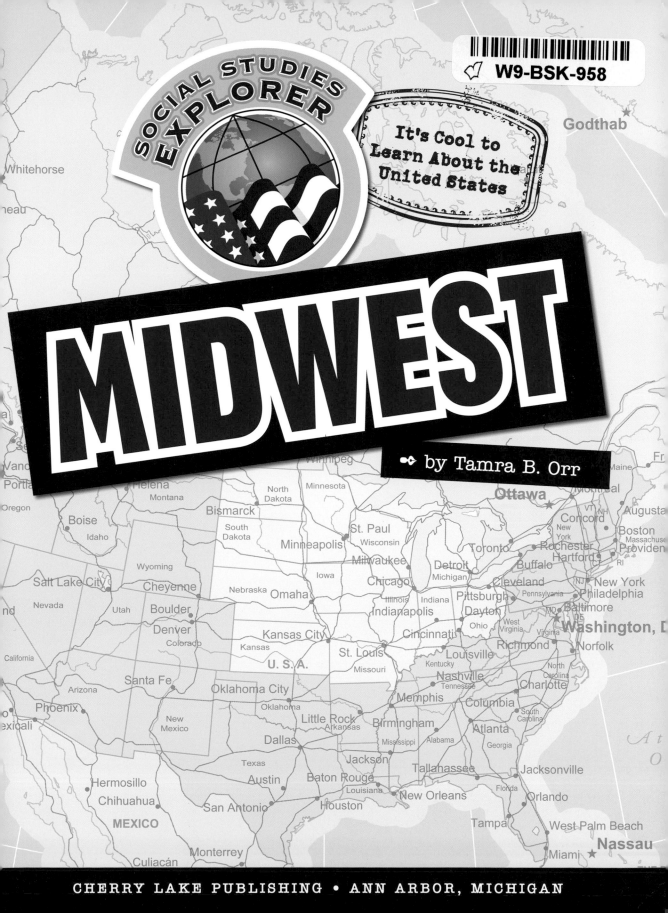

SOCIAL STUDIES EXPLORER

It's Cool to Learn About the United States

MIDWEST

↠ by Tamra B. Orr

CHERRY LAKE PUBLISHING · ANN ARBOR, MICHIGAN

Published in the United States of America
by Cherry Lake Publishing
Ann Arbor, Michigan
www.cherrylakepublishing.com

Content Adviser: James Wolfinger, PhD, Associate Professor,
History and Teacher Education, DePaul University, Chicago, Illinois

Book design: The Design Lab

Photo credits: Cover and page 1, © Cafebeanzphoto/Dreamstime.com,
©Zeljko Radojko/Shutterstock, Inc., ©iofoto/Shutterstock, Inc., and
©Csongor Tari/Shutterstock, Inc.; page 4, ©William Milner/Shutterstock,
Inc.; page 5, ©Ffooter/Shutterstock, Inc.; page 6, ©Rxr3rxr3/Dreamstime.
com; page 7, ©Rudi1976/Dreamstime.com; page 8, ©Carroteater/
Dreamstime.com; page 9, ©GREG RYAN/Alamy and ©Andrew Jalbert/
Shutterstock, Inc.; page 10, ©leonid_tit/Shutterstock, Inc.; page 11,
©Photomyeye/Dreamstime.com; page 12, ©Alexander Podshivalov/
Dreamstime.com; page 13, ©Twildlife/Dreamstime.com; page 15, ©Lyroky/
Alamy; pages 16 and 17, ©North Wind Picture Archives/Alamy; and
page 18, ©Bruce Works/Shutterstock, Inc.; pages 21 and 38, ©Media
Bakery; page 22, ©James Bushelle/Dreamstime.com; page 24, ©Visions
of America, LLC/Alamy; page 25, ©Csehák Szabolcs/Shutterstock, Inc.;
page 26, ©Chunli Li/Dreamstime.com; page 27, ©Ben Lê/Media Bakery;
page 28, ©Andorapro/Dreamstime.com; page 29, ©North Wind Picture
Archives/Alamy; page 30, ©Marvin Dembinsky Photo Associates/Alamy;
page 32, ©LOOK Die Bildagentur der Fotografen GmbH/Alamy; page 33,
©Michael RubinDreamstime.com; page 35, ©Stephen Saks Photography/
Alamy; page 36, ©Grigor Atanasov/Dreamstime.com; page 37, ©Jason P
Ross/Dreamstime.com; page 39, ©Clint Farlinger/Alamy; page 40, ©Joao
Virissimo/Shutterstock, Inc.; page 41, ©Nancy Gill/Shutterstock, Inc.; page
43, ©Elena Talberg/Shutterstock, Inc

Library of Congress Cataloging-in-Publication Data
Orr, Tamra.
   It's cool to learn about the United States: Midwest/by Tamra B. Orr.
      p. cm.—(Social studies explorer)
   Includes bibliographical references and index.
   ISBN-13: 978-1-61080-179-9 (lib. bdg.)
   ISBN-13: 978-1-61080-302-1 (pbk.)
   1. Middle West—Juvenile literature. I. Title. II. Title: Midwest. III. Series.
   F351.O77 2012
   977—dc22   2011004481

Cherry Lake Publishing would like to acknowledge the work
of The Partnership for 21st Century Skills. Please visit
www.21stcenturyskills.org for more information.

Printed in the United States of America
Corporate Graphics Inc.
October 2013
CLFA09

MIDWEST

TABLE OF CONTENTS

USA FIRST-CLASS FOREVER

CHAPTER ONE

WELCOME TO THE MIDWEST

❖ Mount Rushmore is a famous landmark in South Dakota.

Greetings from the Midwest, one of the largest regions in the United States! Twelve states are considered part of the Midwest. They are Illinois, Indiana, Iowa, Kansas, Michigan, Minnesota, Missouri, Nebraska, North Dakota,

Ohio, South Dakota, and Wisconsin. The area has abundant fertile soil and large expanses of flat land. Endless fields of wheat and oats have earned the Midwest its nickname the Nation's Breadbasket.

From the sparkling waters of the Great Lakes to the countless acres of rippling green cornfields, the Midwest is one of America's most scenic regions. Four distinct seasons bring a full range of climates and conditions. The Midwest gets blanketed in thick winter blizzards and is cooled by heavy summer thunderstorms. Spring rains bring buds

The Mackinac Bridge connects the upper and lower peninsulas of the state of Michigan.

bursting forth, and the fall displays a dazzling array of leaves changing to dark gold, burnt orange, and fiery red.

But how did the Midwest get its name? It is located neither in the West nor in the middle of the country. The origin of its name dates to the early years of America's development. At that time, America was made up of 13 colonies located on the East Coast. When Illinois was formed, it was the westernmost land in the growing nation. Colonists began calling that region the "Midwest."

INTO THE CITIES

About one-fifth of the country's population lives in the Midwest. Millions of people live in some of these states' largest cities. Chicago, located in eastern Illinois on Lake Michigan, is the third-largest city in the nation. Cleveland, Ohio, is another large urban area. It is known as the City of Rock and Roll because it is home to the Rock and Roll Hall of Fame and Museum.

↩ Chicago is home to many skyscrapers.

Detroit, Michigan, earned its nickname the Motor City because it is the site of automobile manufacturers such as General Motors, Ford, and Chrysler. Indianapolis, located in central Indiana, is home to the Indy 500, one of the most popular auto races in the world.

▶ Many people visit Indiana to watch races at the Indianapolis Motor Speedway.

Gateway Arch and
the Mall of America

Saint Louis, Missouri, called Gateway City, features a 630-foot (192 meter) shiny silver arch. The arch was completed in 1965 as a monument to the westward expansion of the United States. It is the largest man-made monument in the country. Bloomington, Minnesota, is home to the Mall of America, one of North America's largest malls. It has 520 stores, more than 12,000 parking spaces, an aquarium, and an indoor theme park.

THE WEATHER REPORT

Ask people in the Midwest about their weather and often, even before they can describe it, the weather has changed! The northernmost states experience the coldest temperatures. In wintertime, the states that border the Great Lakes are often buried under "lake effect" snow-falls. States in the southeastern part of the region frequently get a lot of precipitation coming in from the Gulf of Mexico. But it tends to be rain rather than snow.

In summertime, the weather in this region is warm and humid. Thunderstorms are common, bringing brief, hard rains and countless flashes of lightning. Spring months are typically mild, with just enough rain to make the many flowers bloom. Autumn is crisp and cool, helping the leaves put on their autumn show.

➥ Thunderstorms bring the rain necessary for midwest crops to grow.

❖ Hummingbirds can hover in mid-air by flapping their wings quickly.

WILDLIFE

The Midwest is home to all kinds of wildlife. Many kinds of animals live in the region's forests. A wide variety of flowers and green plants can be found in gardens and fields. One of the flowers found growing throughout the region is the coral-colored columbine. The electric orange flowers of the butterfly weed attract all types of butterflies and hummingbirds. Blue sage is a delicate prairie flower. When the flowers grow close together, they make the prairie look sky blue. Unusual plants include the

→ Cows are just one kind of animal raised for food in the Midwest.

jack-in-the-pulpit, which produces berry clusters in the fall. The compass plant has yellow, sunflower-shaped blooms that sit on top of huge, 9-foot (2.7 m) stems. It earned its name because it always grows toward the south.

The farms and forests of the Midwest **abound** with creatures of all types. Farmers raise herds of cattle, sheep, pigs, and even llamas. Forests stir with bears,

elk, deer, moose, coyotes, bobcats, opossums, and badgers. Countless species of frogs, lizards, and snakes are found there. Woodpeckers, meadowlarks, and sparrows live in and around Midwest lakes and ponds. The marbled godwit, a large shorebird, is often found near marshes and ponds. The Sprague's pipit prefers the wide-open grasses found in the flatlands of this region.

Midwestern forests are home to bobcats and many other animals.

ACTIVITY

Look at the map of the Midwest region. Can you name each state capital? Match each city to its state.

1. Indianapolis
2. Madison
3. Bismarck
4. Saint Paul
5. Jefferson City
6. Lincoln
7. Columbus
8. Lansing
9. Pierre
10. Topeka
11. Des Moines
12. Springfield

a. North Dakota
b. Indiana
c. Michigan
d. Minnesota
e. Wisconsin
f. Ohio
g. Nebraska
h. South Dakota
i. Missouri
j. Kansas
k. Illinois
l. Iowa

STOP
Don't write in this book!

Answers: 1-b; 2-e; 3-a; 4-d; 5-i; 6-g; 7-f; 8-c; 9-h; 10-j; 11-l; 12-k

14

CHAPTER TWO

A FINE PLACE TO SETTLE

of plains Indians.

Blades an
working

ring sh

⚬ These Native American artifacts can be seen at Pipestone National Monument in Minnesota.

Native Americans were the first peoples to settle in the Midwest region. Experts have found native **artifacts** dating back more than 1,000 years. Many of these artifacts were discovered in piles of stone and dirt known as

mounds. These mounds were built by a variety of Indian groups, including the Ojibwa and the Sioux. The mounds contained many of the dishes and other items the native peoples used on a daily basis. By the mid-17th century, the Ojibwa and Sioux had settled in areas throughout Minnesota, Wisconsin, and Michigan. The Sioux tribes tended to live in the Great Plains where they could easily hunt buffalo across the flat terrain.

◆▸ Buffalo provided food and clothing for the Plains Indians.

→ Native Americans traded furs, such as beaver pelts, with Europeans.

ARRIVAL OF THE EUROPEANS

By the end of the 17th century, French soldiers, **missionaries**, and fur traders had moved into the region. They set up fur trading posts and missions. The French traded for furs trapped by Native Americans. The furs were sent back to Europe where they were made into clothing for the wealthy. In exchange, the native peoples received metal tools, cloth, and other items made in Europe. French posts and missions were established along the

◆ The fertile farmland of the Midwest attracted many settlers.

Mississippi River and the Great Lakes, where canoes and ships full of cargo could easily dock and load or unload their goods.

In the mid-1700s, England and France fought for control of North America. In 1763, England won the conflict, called the French and Indian War, or the Seven Years' War. From that time on, more settlers from Great Britain began to arrive in the region. The French continued to spread throughout areas west of the Mississippi River.

DATES OF MIDWEST STATEHOOD

States in the Midwest officially achieved statehood on the following dates:

	STATE	DATE OF STATEHOOD	STATE NUMBER
	Ohio	March 1, 1803	17th
	Indiana	December 11, 1816	19th
	Illinois	December 3, 1818	21st
	Missouri	August 10, 1821	24th
	Michigan	January 26, 1837	26th
	Iowa	December 28, 1846	29th
	Wisconsin	May 29, 1848	30th
	Minnesota	May 11, 1858	32nd
	Kansas	January 29, 1861	34th
	Nebraska	March 1, 1867	37th
	North Dakota	November 2, 1889	39th *
	South Dakota	November 2, 1889	40th *

* No one knows which was admitted first. President Benjamin Harrison refused to tell the order in which he signed the two statehood bills.

Determined explorers started moving away from the river's shores and ventured inland. Military forts and trading posts were built. Slowly, people began to explore and settle more of this rich land. By the middle of the 19th century, farmers were coming to the region in greater numbers than traders. Immigrants from Germany headed to eastern Missouri. Immigrants from Sweden and Norway moved into Wisconsin and Minnesota.

HERE COMES THE TRAIN— AND THE STREETCAR

The expansion of the railroad system enabled people to move throughout the Midwest. The railroads also enabled farmers to bring their goods to faraway regions in the country. At the beginning of the 20th century, many midwestern cities were connected by **interurbans,** or electric streetcars. Interurban systems had different names in each state. Throughout northern Indiana, they were called the South Shore Line. In Michigan they were the Detroit United Railway. In Wisconsin the line was called the Milwaukee Electric Railway and Light Company. Traveling on an interurban was quite popular until they were replaced in the 1920s and 1930s with buses.

➥ Buses are a common form of transportation in large Midwestern cities.

As time passed, each of the midwestern states began branching out and developing specialties in farming. Crops grew, and fields expanded so that harvests could be shared, traded, and exported to other states. As towns grew into large cities, an increasing number of tourists came to the area. They spent time in resorts such as the Grand Hotel on Mackinac Island in Michigan.

Industries moved into the states, bringing more jobs and more people. The arrival of the automobile industries helped that expansion. Soon the Midwest had some of the largest cities in the world. People from all over the United States, and even from other countries, moved to make the Midwest their home.

The Grand Hotel on Mackinac Island was built in 1887.

MATCH THE MIDWESTERNERS

Try to match the midwesterner with his or her "claim to fame."

NAME	ACCOMPLISHMENT AND HOME STATE
1. Toni Morrison	a. Sauk Native American leader, born in Illinois
2. Charles Schulz	b. Author also known as Samuel Clemens, born in Missouri
3. Frank Lloyd Wright	c. Escape artist and magician, born in Michigan
4. Mark Twain	d. Actor in western movies, born in Iowa
5. Black Hawk	e. Author of Little House on the Prairie series, born in Wisconsin
6. Harry Houdini	f. Pulitzer Prize winner for literature in 1988, born in Ohio
7. John Wayne	g. Popular singer and performer, born in Indiana
8. Laura Ingalls Wilder	h. 31st U.S. president, born in Iowa
9. Michael Jackson	i. Creator of Peanuts cartoons, born in Minnesota
10. Herbert Hoover	j. American architect and interior designer, born in Wisconsin

Answers: 1-f; 2-i; 3-j; 4-b; 5-a; 6-c; 7-d; 8-e; 9-g; 10-h

CHAPTER THREE

IN AMERICA'S BREADBASKET

⚬ Many pioneers lived in cabins like this one in South Dakota.

In search of a new life, American pioneers and immigrants arrived in the region. They discovered an abundance of sunshine and rain, and millions of acres of rich soil. It was a perfect combination of natural elements,

one that helped farmers establish agriculture as the Midwest's main industry.

Today midwestern farmers produce huge amounts of wheat and corn. They ship these crops throughout the nation and to many countries around the world. The corn is harvested and used to make many types of foods, as well as other products such as glue, soap, and paint. Kansas and North Dakota grow large quantities of wheat. It is usually ground into flour and then used to make foods such as cakes, bread, and noodles. In

➻ Wheat is an important crop in the Midwest.

→ Some Midwestern farmers raise bison for their meat.

addition to corn and wheat, the Midwest is also known for growing crops such as oats, barley, soybeans, sunflowers, and flaxseed.

Many farmers have large cattle ranches. They supply beef to local and national markets. Minnesota, Wisconsin, and Michigan have perfected the science of breeding cows. They use them to produce dairy products that include cheese, milk, and butter. Bison ranches are becoming popular. These large animals require less care and live longer than cattle but still produce large amounts of meat.

TAKING CARE OF BUSINESS

The Midwest is home to many large and **diverse** businesses. Michigan is a leading manufacturer of automobiles and automobile parts. Nebraska is considered a center for insurance companies. Minnesota's largest cities include Minneapolis, home of the world's largest supercomputer, and Saint Paul, site of the nation's third-largest trucking center. Wichita, Kansas, is a major producer of private aircraft. Iowa is known for its lumber products. Chicago is a major world financial center

◆◆ The company that builds Cessna airplanes is headquartered in Wichita, Kansas.

and world **convention** destination. Manufacturers in Cincinnati, Ohio, makes jet engines and machine tools.

Indiana is a major producer of steel, coal, and limestone. Wisconsin's mines produce large amounts of copper, iron, lead, and zinc. North Dakota produces farm equipment, and South Dakota produces more sunflower seeds than almost any other state in the nation. Missouri manufacturers supply many types of transportation equipment.

↝ Coal production is a big part of Indiana's economy.

●➔ The Little White Schoolhouse in Ripon, Wisconsin, is the birthplace of the Republican Party.

POLITICS AND GOVERNMENT

The Midwest has a long history of involvement in U.S. politics. The Republican Party got its start in Wisconsin 160 years ago. One of its top **priorities** was to put an end to slavery. This region of the country also helped jump-start the Progressive movement, a period of social activism and political reform that was popular from the 1890s to 1920s. Midwestern farmers and business owners contributed greatly to the goals of the Progressives.

In modern-day presidential elections, midwestern states are often referred to as swing states. They are

➤ A crowd gathers at a Tea Party protest in Michigan.

also called battleground states. These are states where no single candidate or political party has enough support to consistently secure that state's electoral votes. Swing states, therefore, are major targets for political parties to campaign. The area has seen many protests by the Tea Party, which began protesting in New York in 2009. The Tea Party tends to be a politically conservative group, taking its name from the Boston Tea Party of 1773.

Like the other regions of the country, each one of the midwestern states is run by an elected governor who serves for 4 years. In addition, the cities within each state have mayors, whose terms vary from one state to the other. Most terms run between 2 and 4 years.

ACTIVITY

TOP FIVE MIDWESTERN WHEAT-PRODUCING STATES

Graphs can be a great way to compare things. Using the information below, make a bar graph to show the number of bushels of wheat these midwestern states produced in 2005.

STATE	BUSHELS (IN MILLIONS)
North Dakota	380,000
Kansas	374,000
South Dakota	133,400
Minnesota	71,500
Nebraska	68,600

CHAPTER FOUR

FOLKS, FOOD, AND FUN

❧ People of many different ethnicities enjoy a dance festival in Chicago.

Midwesterners are a mix of ethnicities. They live in small towns and huge urban cities as well as on family farms and sprawling ranches. The Midwest's early appeal to immigrant groups had led to large numbers

of German, Irish, English, and African American settlers. There is also a growing population of Hispanic Americans.

The population of the Midwest is about 67 million. Illinois has the region's largest population with 12.9 million people living there. It has the fifth-largest state population in the country. Ohio, with large cities such as Cleveland and Cincinnati, is ranked seventh nationally with a population of 11.5 million.

Hispanic American girls participate in a Cinco de Mayo parade in St. Paul, Minnesota.

STATE	POPULATION	% CHANGE 2000-2009	NATIONAL RANK
Illinois	12.9 million	4.0	5th
Ohio	11.5 million	1.7	7th
Michigan	9.9 million	0.3	8th
Indiana	6.4 million	5.6	16th
Missouri	5.9 million	7.0	18th
Wisconsin	5.6 million	5.4	20th
Minnesota	5.2 million	7.0	21st
Iowa	3 million	2.8	30th
Kansas	2.8 million	4.8	33rd
Nebraska	1.8 million	5.0	38th
South Dakota	812,383	7.6	46th
North Dakota	646,844	0.7	48th

COME TO HAVE FUN

The Midwest offers something for everyone who comes to visit or live there. Let's take a tour of the amazing wonders to discover and explore, beginning in Kansas and heading east.

In Kansas, you might stop by Dodge City, an authentic Old West town. It features the Long Branch Saloon, a cowboy burial ground, and an annual rodeo. You could also take a tour of Fort Leavenworth, the oldest active U.S. Army post west of the Mississippi River. In Missouri, stop by Branson to listen to some country-western stars perform. Then take a trip along the Pony Express National Historic Trail. Do not forget to check out Mark Twain's boyhood home in Hannibal.

◈ You can visit the Front Street buildings to learn what life was like in Dodge City in 1876.

Your next stop is Illinois. There you can spend days exploring Chicago's Art Institute, the Museum of Science and Industry, the Shedd Aquarium, and Adler Planetarium. In Indiana, spend an afternoon at the Dunes National Lakeshore to enjoy the water and sun. If you have a "need for speed," stop at the Indianapolis Motor Speedway to check out the latest races. In Ohio, walk through the Rock and Roll Hall of Fame and Museum. You can also spend some time learning about Native American life at the Indian burial grounds at the Mound City Group National Monument.

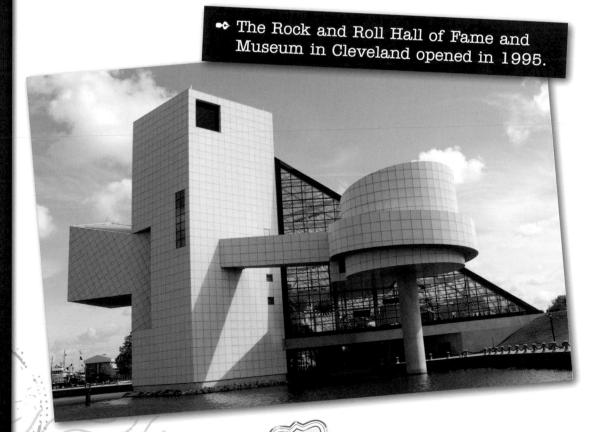

The Rock and Roll Hall of Fame and Museum in Cleveland opened in 1995.

◆◇ Visit the Wisconsin Dells to see many beautiful rock formations.

Michigan offers a relaxing afternoon at the Mackinac Island resort. If you're the adventurous type, explore the endless water fun that can be found on all of the Great Lakes. Stop in Wisconsin and spend your day admiring the beautiful sandstone formations of the Wisconsin Dells. Then enjoy a stop at the Circus World Museum before you take a boat ride on Winnebago, one of the 14,000 lakes found in this state.

● South Dakota's Corn Palace attracts about 500,000 visitors each year.

In the winter, Minnesota hosts the Saint Paul Winter Carnival. In warmer months, you can take a stroll through the Minnesota Zoo. A trip to North Dakota means a tour through Badlands National Park. There you can see fossils of prehistoric animals and amazing scenery. In South Dakota, everyone stops by the World's Only Corn Palace, where everything you see, touch, and eat is about corn. For fans of the Old West, mosey into the city of Deadwood, where Wild Bill Hickok was killed in 1876.

In Iowa, take a step back in time at the Amana Colonies. People in this group of several small villages specialize in making handmade goods and living the way people lived a century ago. Find out more about Indian mounds at the Effigy Mounds National Monument, a prehistoric Indian burial site. Finish your journey in Nebraska where you can learn about prehistoric times with a trip to the Agate Fossil Beds.

•❖ You can see ancient Native American burial mounds at Effigy Mounds National Monument in Iowa.

COME TO EAT

Midwestern food is not typically gourmet or exotic, but it is delicious. In summer months, some of the most common treats that show up at picnics are potato salad, deviled eggs, and green bean casserole. Meat loaf, barbecued chicken, steak, and hot dogs on the grill are midwestern favorites, too. They are often served with an ear of corn on the side. Many farmers' wives bake their own bread.

➥ Hot dogs and other grilled foods are Midwestern favorites.

❧ Whether visiting a farm or big city, the Midwest has something for everyone.

The Midwest has a unique blend of history, cultural experiences, rural and urban destinations, and breathtaking natural beauty. They all add up to make it one of the nation's most appealing regions to residents and visitors alike.

The Midwest is known for the acres of sweet corn it grows. Here is a great recipe using some of that summer bounty. These fritters can be a side dish, a snack, or even the appetizer at a weekend barbecue. Be sure to ask an adult to help you cut and fry the ingredients.

Sweet Corn Fritters

INGREDIENTS
2 large ears fresh sweet corn
   (or 1 packed cup frozen corn, thawed and drained)
2 large eggs
$\frac{1}{4}$ cup whole milk
$\frac{1}{4}$ cup all-purpose flour
3 tablespoons yellow cornmeal
$1\frac{1}{2}$ teaspoons sugar
$\frac{1}{2}$ teaspoon salt
$2\frac{1}{2}$ teaspoons baking powder
Canola oil for frying

→ For the freshest tasting corn fritters, have an adult help you cut the kernels off cobs of corn.

INSTRUCTIONS

1. Have an adult cut the corn kernels off of the cob into a large bowl.
2. Whisk the eggs and milk into the corn until completely combined.
3. In a separate bowl, combine the flour, cornmeal, sugar, salt, and baking powder.
4. Pour the dry ingredients into the bowl of corn and stir to create a thick batter.
5. Pour oil about ³/₄ inch deep into a heavy-duty skillet. Have the heat on medium.
6. When the oil is hot, have an adult drop rounded tablespoons of batter into it. Make sure the fritters do not touch each other.
7. Cook for 3 minutes on each side, until all sides are golden brown.
8. Drain on paper towels and serve immediately.

FAST FACTS

Population of region (2009): 66,836,911

Total area of region: 766,363 square miles (1,984,871 sq km)

Highest point: 7,242 feet (2,207 m) Harney Peak, South Dakota

Lowest point: 230 feet (70 m) Saint Francis River, Missouri

Highest recorded temperature: 118°F (47.8°C) in Keokuk, Iowa, on July 20, 1934

Lowest recorded temperature: -54°F (-47.8°C) in Danbury, Wisconsin, on January 24, 1922

Largest cities (2009): Chicago, Illinois (2,851,268); Detroit, Michigan (910,920); Indianapolis, Indiana (807,584)

Professional Sports Teams:

Major League Baseball: Chicago Cubs, Chicago White Sox, Cincinnati Reds, Cleveland Indians, Detroit Tigers, Kansas City Royals, Milwaukee Brewers, Minnesota Twins, and Saint Louis Cardinals

Major League Soccer: Chicago Fire, Columbus Crew, and Sporting Kansas City

National Basketball Association: Chicago Bulls, Cleveland Cavaliers, Detroit Pistons, Indiana Pacers, Milwaukee Bucks, and Minnesota Timberwolves

National Football League: Chicago Bears, Cincinnati Bengals, Cleveland Browns, Detroit Lions, Green Bay Packers, Indianapolis Colts, Kansas City Chiefs, Minnesota Vikings, and Saint Louis Rams

National Hockey League: Chicago Blackhawks, Columbus Blue Jackets, Detroit Red Wings, Minnesota Wild, and Saint Louis Blues

GLOSSARY

abound (uh-BOUND) to have a large amount of something

artifacts (ART-uh-fakts) objects made by human beings, such as weapons or tools from the past

convention (kuhn-VEN-shun) a large gathering of people who have the same interests

diverse (di-VURS) varied or assorted

interurbans (in-tuhr-UR-buhnz) electric streetcars popular in the Midwest until the 1920s and 1930s

missionaries (MISH-uh-ner-eez) people who are sent to a foreign country to teach a religious faith

mounds (MOUNDZ) prehistoric earthworks raised over graves, often used in Native American cultures

priorities (prye-OR-uh-teez) things that are more important or urgent than other things